Following Jesus

James Jones

with illustrations by
Taffy

1 Is there a God?

2 I can't see God

3 Was Jesus the Son of God?

4 What is faith?

5 What is a Christian?

6 Getting ready for Jesus (Mark 1)

7 How do I start following Jesus?

8 A follower of Jesus (Mark 2)

9 Turning to Christ

10 A family of followers (Mark 3)

11 How should I behave as a follower of Jesus?

12 Following Jesus at home

13 Keep on following (Mark 4)

14 How should I pray?

15 What should I pray for?

16 Is prayer just coincidence?

17 Following Jesus can be lonely (Mark 6)

18 Do I have to go to church?

19 Belonging to the Church

20 The heart of the follower (Mark 7)

21 The followers realize who Jesus is (Mark 8)

22 Is the Bible reliable?

23 The Bible as God's word

24 In the master's service (Mark 10)

25 Jesus is king (Mark 11)

26 Jesus' two commandments (Mark 12)

27 Jesus tells the future (Mark 13)

28 Holy Communion—with Jesus (Mark 14)

29 Holy Communion—with each other

30 Jesus dies and rises (Mark 15 & 16)

31 Jesus and the Holy Spirit

ship

1

A famous scientist had a model of the universe on his desk. It was very impressive with the planets going round the sun. One day a friend who didn't believe in God saw it. He liked it so much he wanted one for himself. He asked the scientist who had made it. Now the scientist did believe in God and thought that he would have a bit of fun with his friend. 'What do you mean?', he said. 'Who made it? What a silly question! Nobody made it. It just appeared here. Out of nowhere.' The friend got angry. 'Come off it', he shouted, 'Don't be stupid. Things don't just appear like that. Somebody must have made it.' The scientist paused and smiled. 'You're right', he said, 'Somebody did make it. But listen my friend. You refused to believe that this model could have happened without a maker. Why then do you believe that the real universe—billions times greater—could exist without a creator?'

 Read what Paul said in his letter to the Christians in Rome:

God punishes them, because what can be known about God is plain to them, for God himself made it plain. Ever since God created the world, his invisible qualities, both his eternal power and his divine nature, have been clearly seen; they are perceived in the things that God has made. So those people have no excuse at all!

Romans 1:19, 20

OF COURSE NO ONE MADE THIS MODEL – IT JUST HAPPENED!

Is there a God?

You may have started to wonder if there really is a God. Perhaps you know people who tell you they don't believe in God. It's difficult to argue with them. We can't all be as clever as the scientist. But look at the world. Look at nature. Look at the animals—the cheetah, the elephant, the hamster. They've been beautifully made. There's nothing silly about believing that somebody must have made them. And that somebody, so the Bible tells us, is God.

P.S. In an American opinion poll it was discovered that at least seven out of every ten scientists believed in God.

Lord God, it's hard to argue with people who don't believe in you. And sometimes I begin to wonder whether you are really there. But when I look at all the beautiful things in the world I can't help thinking that you must have made them all. Help me to be sure. And help me to understand those who don't believe. Amen

At your Confirmation the Bishop will ask you:
'Do you believe and trust in God the Father who made the world?'

You will answer:
'I believe and trust in him.'

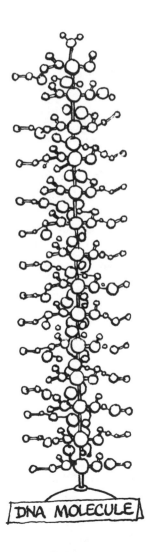

DNA MOLECULE

One of the problems about believing in God is that we can't see him. Maybe you've said to yourself, 'If only I could see him I'd believe in him'.

Here's a story to think about. A man set sail in his yacht to travel round the world. The wind filled his sails and sent him on his way. One day in the middle of the Pacific Ocean he woke up to find that there was no wind. In the distance he could see a beautiful island and paddled towards it. There were people standing on the beach. The man was frightened. But when he saw their smiling faces and waving arms he smiled and waved back. There was something strange about the island. To his surprise he found that although they spoke different languages they could understand each other perfectly.

The islanders asked the man how long it had taken him to paddle across the ocean. The man laughed and said he had used his sails. The islanders looked puzzled. Sails? What are they? The man pointed to the sagging white and red sails and explained how fast the boat went when they were full of a strong wind. Wind? The islanders looked even more puzzled. What is this wind? What does it look like? How big is it? Where does it come from? Now it was the man's turn to look amazed. Doesn't the wind ever blow on this island? They looked at each other puzzled. The islanders didn't know what he was talking about. They had never come across wind.

I can't
see God

How could the man explain to them what wind was? How could he even prove to these islanders that such a thing as wind even existed . . . ?

How would you go about it? Perhaps you could finish the story. We can't see the wind and we can't see God. Both are invisible. We know the wind is there when we see the effect it has on things like trees and sails. We know that God is there when we see the effect he has on people like Mother Teresa. She shows God's love to those she helps.

Read what John, one of Jesus' disciples, wrote to some Christian friends:
Dear friends, if this is how God loved us, then we should love one another. No one has ever seen God, but if we love one another, God lives in union with us, and his love is made perfect in us.

1 John 4:11, 12

Dear Lord, thank you that even though I can't see you I can see the effect you have on people. Help me to love others so that they can see your love in me. Help me to be someone who shows others that you are really there. Amen.

3

Was Jesus the Son of God?

Imagine: the news on TV tonight: 'A man claiming to be God's Son arrived in London today . . .'

What would you expect him to be like if he really was God's Son? Put a tick by 'Yes' or 'No'.

He would be kind.	'Yes'	'No'
He would be firm.	'Yes'	'No'
He would love his enemies.	'Yes'	'No'
He would heal people.	'Yes'	'No'
He would forgive people.	'Yes'	'No'
He would stand up for the weak.	'Yes'	'No'
He would, if killed, come back to life.	'Yes'	'No'
He would teach people to be good.	'Yes'	'No'
He would work miracles	'Yes'	'No'
(not just for fun but to help people).		

If the man did all the things you've marked 'Yes', you would probably join the crowds that would flock to see him.

Well, 2000 years ago there was a man who was like that. He had a tick by 'Yes' nine times. He was so special that thousands of people wanted to see him. It was clear to many of them that he was more than just a good man. In the end what proved to his followers that Jesus really was the Son of God was his Resurrection. After being killed he came back to life. Even then it was hard for some of them to believe.

 Read how John described it:

One of the twelve disciples, Thomas (called the Twin), was not with them when Jesus came. So the other disciples told him, 'We have seen the Lord!' Thomas said to them, 'Unless I see the scars of the nails in his hands and put my finger on those scars and my hand in his side, I will not believe.' A week later the disciples were together again indoors, and Thomas was with them. The doors were locked, but Jesus came and stood among them and said, 'Peace be with you.' Then he said to Thomas, 'Put your finger here, and look at my hands; then stretch out your hand and put it in my side. Stop your doubting and believe!' Thomas answered him, 'My Lord and my God!' Jesus said to him, 'Do you believe because you have seen me? How happy are those who believe without seeing me!'

John 20:24–29

Like Thomas we may find the Resurrection hard to believe. But we would be more surprised if the Son of God did not rise from the dead. We should expect God's Son to be able to come back from the dead.

Lord Jesus, you know how hard it is to believe without having seen you. Thank you that we have the Bible so that we can get to know you. Thank you that we have other Christians in the Church who can help us to understand. You are 'my Lord and my God.' Help me to follow you. Amen.

4

What is faith?

Imagine you threw a kite and it got caught in a tree. The only way you could get it down was by climbing on to a friend's shoulders and reaching through the branches. You would have to have a lot of faith in your friend. You would have to trust that he wouldn't walk away or let you fall. That's faith. Trusting someone else.

Here are some other words that have similar meaning. Perhaps you could unscramble them:
GYERLNI
PDENIDGEN
NALENIG

When the Bible uses the word faith it talks about having or putting your faith in God and in Jesus. It means simply 'depending on God', 'depending on Jesus'.
The Bible is full of stories about men and women who depend on God. Sadly we don't depend on God enough. And very often we only start to rely on God when things in our life go wrong. What is amazing is that God never gives up on us and is longing to help us. The Gospels show us people putting their faith in and depending on Jesus. Some depended on him to heal them. Some depended on him to forgive them. A Christian is someone who *depends* on Jesus, who *has faith* in Jesus, who *trusts* in Jesus.

Read Mark 10:46–52 about blind Bartimaeus:

They came to Jericho, and as Jesus was leaving with his disciples and a large crowd, a blind beggar named Bartimaeus son of Timaeus was sitting by the road. When he heard that it was Jesus of Nazareth, he began to shout, 'Jesus! Son of David! Take pity on me!' Many of the people scolded him and told him to be quiet. But he shouted even more loudly, 'Son of David, take pity on me!' Jesus stopped and said, 'Call him.' So they called the blind man. 'Cheer up!' they said. 'Get up, he is calling you.' He threw off his cloak, jumped up, and came to Jesus. 'What do you want me to do for you?' Jesus asked him. 'Teacher,' the blind man answered, 'I want to see again.' 'Go,' Jesus told him, 'your faith has made you well.' At once he was able to see and followed Jesus on the road.

At the end Jesus says, 'Your faith has made you well,' Put that sentence in a different way using one of the scrambled words.

Lord Jesus, the blind man trusted you to help him. I trust you to help me too. Amen.

5

Read what John says:

For God loved the world so much that he gave his only Son, so that everyone who believes in him may not die but have eternal life.

John 3:16

A Christian is someone who has faith in Jesus. He trusts in him and depends on him. The Church, which stretches all over the world, is made up of all those who depend on Jesus. To be a Christian means therefore that we belong to the Church.

God wants us to live always in his presence. Sadly, all of us shut God out of our lives when we refuse to depend on him. Just like a plant can't go on living without water, so you and I can't have any life that's worth living without God. To shut God out of our lives is very serious. It's a sin that hurts God badly. But God never gives up loving us. He always wants to forgive us. That's why he sent Jesus into the world.

When Jesus died on the cross, he took away the sins of the world. He offers us forgiveness for the sins that shut God out. He destroys the wall that blocks us off from God. And so he makes it possible for us to live with God forever.

A Christian is someone who depends on Jesus Christ for forgiveness and eternal life.

Lord Jesus, I know I'm often selfish. I know it hurts you. But thank you for still loving me. Forgive me and help me to follow you. Amen.

 At your Confirmation the Bishop will ask you:

'Do you believe and trust in his Son Jesus Christ, who redeemed mankind?'

You will answer:
'I believe and trust in him.'

What is a Christian?

Imagine for a moment living in a country where there were no water taps! What difference would it make to your life? Make a list here of all the things you use water for:

....

....

....

In the time of Jesus some people would go to the river Jordan for a bath. It was a good way of washing dirt from your body.

But when John the Baptist came and dipped people in the river Jordan he was doing more than giving them a bath.

 Read Mark 1:1–4

This is the Good News about Jesus Christ, the Son of God. It began as the prophet Isaiah had written: 'God said, "I will send my messenger ahead of you to clear the way for you." Someone is shouting in the desert, "Get the road ready for the Lord; make a straight path for him to travel!"' So John appeared in the desert, baptizing and preaching. 'Turn away from your sins and be baptized,' he told the people, 'and God will forgive your sins.'

By baptizing them John was getting people ready for Jesus. Dipping them in the water was a picture that God was washing their sins away. They were now clean, forgiven and ready for following Jesus.

Because we're all sinners we all need to be baptized as a sign that our sins are forgiven.

Preparing for Confirmation is like getting ready to follow Jesus. But first you'll need to be baptized for the forgiveness of your sins.

Lord Jesus, thank you for giving us baptism as such a clear picture of the way you wash away our sins. Thank you for giving us a new start. Amen.

P.S. If you've not been baptized, talk to your minister about it. He or she will tell you more about what it means.

Getting ready for Jesus

7

Becoming a Christian means deciding for yourself to follow Jesus.

 Listen to what Jesus said:

> Then Jesus called the crowd and his disciples to him. 'If anyone wants to come with me,' he told them, 'he must forget self, carry his cross, and follow me.'
>
> Mark 8:34

'Forget self' means being unselfish.

Take a few moments now to think of the times today or yesterday when you've seen somebody being selfish.
Now take some time to think of the moments when you've been selfish.
How hard would you have found it to be unselfish?
Jesus knows that it's very hard to 'forget self'. That's why he said it would be like taking up a cross. It would be difficult and painful.

 **At your Confirmation the Bishop will ask you:**
'Do you repent of (turn away from) your sins?'

You will answer:
'I repent of my sins.'

In saying this you're promising to make the effort not to be selfish. When you're tempted to put yourself first, stop and think 'What would Jesus do if he were in my shoes?'

Heavenly Father,
I have sinned against you
Through my own fault
In thought and word and deed,
And in what I have left undone.
For your Son our Lord Jesus Christ's sake,
Forgive me all that is past;
And grant that I may serve you in newness of life. Amen.

How do I start following Jesus?

Many people think that Christianity is just for good people. They couldn't be more wrong! Jesus came specially for people who knew they weren't any good. He came to help poor people and bad people, people who had no friends and did things wrong every day of their lives. He was like a doctor helping sick patients. Some of the most hated and lonely people of his time were tax collectors. Jesus came to help them too.

 Read Mark 2:13–17

Jesus went back again to the shore of Lake Galilee. A crowd came to him, and he started teaching them. As he walked along, he saw a tax collector, Levi son of Alphaeus, sitting in his office. Jesus said to him, 'Follow me.' Levi got up and followed him. Later on Jesus was having a meal in Levi's house. A large number of tax collectors and other outcasts were following Jesus, and many of them joined him and his disciples at the table. Some teachers of the Law, who were Pharisees, saw that Jesus was eating with these outcasts and tax collectors, so they asked his disciples, 'Why does he eat with such people?' Jesus heard them and answered, 'People who are well do not need a doctor, but only those who are sick. I have not come to call respectable people, but outcasts.'

Tax collectors were hated by the Jews because they cheated. They took too much money and lined their own pockets. Yet Jesus made friends with tax collectors. He even asked Levi (also known as Matthew) to be one of his closest followers.

Jesus spoke out against stealing and doing wrong things. But he still loved the people who did them. He told them they had to stop what they were doing and turn their back on evil.

 At your Confirmation the Bishop will ask you:
'Do you renounce (turn your back on) evil?'

You will answer:
'I renounce evil.'

Take a moment to think of what you will turn your back on.

It could mean breaking away from a gang who bully people. It could mean standing up for someone who gets bullied at school. It could mean giving up lying, or stealing or cheating. It could mean giving up swearing at people. It could mean trying to be helpful at home.

9

Turning to Christ

Turning your back on evil and turning over a new leaf are difficult things to do. Without Christ's help it would be impossible for us to keep it up. By turning to Christ we can get help. Because he is alive and with us today we can ask him to come into our lives and help us.

 Many years after the Resurrection those in the church at Laodicea received a message from God. He said how much he loved them and how he longed to change them. Then he said:

I rebuke and punish all whom I love. Be in earnest, then, and turn from your sins. Listen! I stand at the door and knock; if anyone hears my voice and opens the door, I will come into his house and eat with him, and he will eat with me.

Revelation 3:19, 20

 At your Confirmation the Bishop will ask you:
'Do you turn to Christ?'

You will answer:
'I turn to Christ.'

By turning to Christ in this way we can know him not just as our example but as a friend who lives within us to help us.

Lord Jesus, you know everything about me. You know that I need to change. Forgive me for all my sins. I turn to you and ask you to come to me as you've promised. Help me to follow your example and to live like you. Amen.

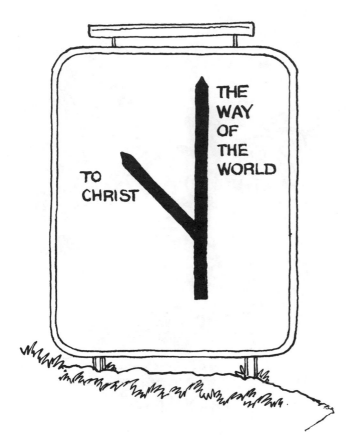

TO CHRIST

THE
WAY
OF
THE
WORLD

10

A family
of followers

Jesus belonged to a family. He had a mother and a father and lots of brothers and sisters. One day his family came to see him, all except Joseph who had died.

Read Mark 3:31–35

Then Jesus' mother and brothers arrived. They stood outside the house and sent in a message, asking for him. A crowd was sitting round Jesus, and they said to him, 'Look, your mother and your brothers and sisters are outside, and they want you.' Jesus answered, 'Who is my mother? Who are my brothers?' He looked at the people sitting round him and said, 'Look! Here are my mother and my brothers! Whoever does what God wants him to do is my brother, my sister, my mother.'

In fact, Jesus belonged to two families. The one that he was born into and the other that was made up of all the people who do God's will.

As a follower of Jesus you too belong to two families. The one you were born or adopted into and the other which is the family of Jesus.

The family of Jesus is made up of those who follow Jesus and want to do God's will.

One of the things that God wants us to do as part of his family, is mentioned in the Ten Commandments.

Commandment number five:

Respect your father and your mother.

Exodus 20:12

Just as you can very often tell who's somebody's brother or sister, or mother or father, by what he or she looks like, so you should be able to tell who's in the family of Jesus by the way they live and follow God's commandments.

What sort of things do you think a follower of Jesus should do and shouldn't do? Make two lists here:

Should do   Shouldn't do

. . . .

. . . .

. . . .

. . . .

. . . .

. . . .

. . . .

. . . .

. . . .

11

Paul wrote two letters to the Christians in Corinth. This is part of what he said:

> Love is patient and kind; it is not jealous or conceited or proud; love is not ill-mannered or selfish or irritable; love does not keep a record of wrongs; love is not happy with evil, but is happy with truth. Love never gives up; and its faith, hope, and patience never fail.

1 Corinthians 13:4–7

What's the hardest of all these things to be? Why?

. . . .

. . . .

. . . .

. . . .

. . . .

. . . .

Write the name of Jesus instead of the word 'love'. This will give you a good picture of Jesus.

> ....is patient and kind;................is not jealous or conceited or proud;................is not ill-mannered or selfish or irritable;................does not keep a record of

wrongs;................is not happy with evil, but is happy with the truth................never gives up; and................' faith, hope, and patience never fail.

What examples can you think of when Jesus showed patience and kindness?

. . . .

. . . .

. . . .

. . . .

. . . .

. . . .

God wants us to be like Jesus. So, instead of the word 'Jesus' write in your own name.

> ....is patient and kind;................is not jealous or conceited or proud;................is not ill-mannered or selfish or irritable;................does not keep a record of wrongs;................is not happy with evil, but is happy with the truth................never gives up; and................'s faith, hope, and patience never fail.

It's difficult putting our own names in because it's hard to be like Jesus every single moment of the day.

Lord Jesus, I'm sorry for not being like you. Please forgive me. Help me to think about you more. Help me to become more like you. Help me to be kind and patient today. Amen.

How should I behave as a follower of Jesus?

In what things do you find it most difficult to get on with your parents? Number the following from 1 to 12 in order of difficulty.

Amount of pocket money
Which TV programmes to watch
Washing up rota
Time for getting in at night
Keeping your bedroom clean
Time for going to bed
Clothes you wear
The friends you have
Your school report
Table manners
The music you listen to
Hairstyles

There have always been differences between parents and young people ever since Adam and Eve. And there always will be. When the Bible talks about children honouring their parents it does not mean that children must always like what their parents like. It means that children should respect their parents.

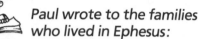

Paul wrote to the families who lived in Ephesus:

Children, it is your Christian duty to obey your parents, for this is the right thing to do. 'Respect your father and mother . . .'

Following

In case that sounds a bit one-sided, Paul added:
Parents, do not treat your children in such a way as to make them angry.

Ephesians 6:1–4

Door-slamming children and nagging parents both get a warning from the Bible.
Parents should try and see how things look from their children's point of view and young people must try and see things from their parents' position.
So the next time you have a disagreement with your parents, stop and think how they feel. You'll still probably have different tastes in music, clothes and hairstyles but as a Christian you'll be trying to live in harmony and not discord.

Lord, you know that it's not easy to be a Christian at home. Forgive me for the times when I lose my temper. Help me to see my parents' viewpoint and help them to see mine too. Thank you for my family. Amen.

Jesus at home

13 Keep on following

Jesus told a famous story. It's called the Parable of the Sower.

Read it for yourself:

 Read Mark 4:1–9

The seed fell on four types of ground. Write them down in the left hand column:

....

....

....

....

Read Mark 4:13–20

Jesus explained what the four different grounds were. Write them down in the second column opposite the correct types.

Put a tick by the sort of ground you think you are.

Put a tick by the sort of ground you would like to be.

Many people who heard Jesus promised to follow him. But when things got difficult they gave up and deserted him.

A lot of people today make promises to follow Jesus, especially at Confirmation, but later on they give up. Make a list here of things that will make it difficult for you to follow Jesus:

. . . .

. . . .

. . . .

. . . .

. . . .

. . . .

Lord Jesus, you know how difficult it is to follow you. It's hard to go to church when your friends are off having a good time somewhere else. It's hard when people make fun of you. You know that I want to follow you to the end. Help me to be like the good soil. Amen.

14

How should I pray?

Praying is 'talking with God'. If you can't think of what to say, try this prayer which Jesus gave us:

One day Jesus was praying in a certain place. When he had finished, one of his disciples said to him, 'Lord, teach us to pray, just as John taught his disciples.' Jesus said to them, 'When you pray, say this:

Father:
May your holy name
be honoured;
may your Kingdom come.
Give us day by day
the food we need.
Forgive us our sins,
for we forgive everyone
who does us wrong.
And do not bring us to
hard testing.'

Luke 11:1–4

Whom should I pray to?

Jesus told us to talk to God as our 'Father'. God loves us like a good father loves his children. (If you've time, look up what Jesus said in Luke 11:5–13.)

When should I pray?

Any time! But it's good to take a special time each day to read the Bible and talk to God. (Jesus prayed in the morning and at night and whenever he had to make a big decision.)

Here's another way of praying the Lord's Prayer:

Dear Father, help us always to look up to you. Make everybody know that you are King of the universe. Please give us all that we need. Forgive us for all our mistakes. Help us to forgive those who've been unkind to us. Please don't make it too hard to follow Jesus.

Put the Lord's prayer into your own words.

....

....

....

....

....

....

P.S. Jesus never orders us to say 'Thank you'. He leaves it to us to say it of our own accord.

Here's something to think about:

Would a parent give a baby a carving knife to play with? Would a parent let a child play with a model before the glue had set? Would a father let his little girl drive the car? Would a mother let her little boy play at the hot cooker?

Of course, the answer is 'No'. Even though the children scream and shout, even though they have tantrums. The good parent won't let them have what they want. Sometimes we ask God for things which he knows aren't good for us. God knows the difference between **what we want** and **what we need**. It takes us a lifetime to find out the difference. So, sometimes our prayers will be answered with a 'No', sometimes with a 'Yes', and sometimes with a 'Not yet'.

Listen to what Paul wrote:

Don't worry about anything, but in all your prayers ask God for what you need, always asking him with a thankful heart. And God's peace, which is far beyond human understanding, will keep your hearts and minds safe in union with Christ Jesus.

Philippians 4:6, 7

Tell God *everything*. Leave it to him to decide what's best for you.

> **P.S. Don't forget to say 'Thank you'.**

Things to ask God for

Things to thank God for

What should I pray for?

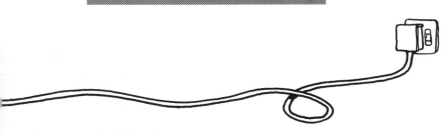

16

When God says 'Yes' to one of our prayers it's a great boost to our faith. We feel like telling the whole world. People who don't follow Jesus sometimes say, 'Oh, it's just a coincidence', and, in a way, they're right. The answer **coincides** with the prayer.

Jesus told us the secret of getting our prayers answered with a 'Yes':

If you remain in me and my words remain in you, then you will ask for anything you wish, and you shall have it.

John 15:7

The secret is knowing what Jesus would ask the Father if he were in our shoes.

It takes a lifetime getting to know what Jesus would ask for. Reading the Bible, and worshipping God with other Christians, especially at Holy Communion, are two important ways of getting on the same wavelength as Jesus and of being at one with him.

As we get to know Jesus better so we get a clearer idea of the sort of prayers to which God gives a 'thumbs up'.

So when you pray, don't rush in with all your requests.

(i) Stop and think about God the Father first. Thank him for giving his Son, Jesus.

(ii) Then as you think about Jesus begin to say how sorry you are for anything bad you've done or said or thought.

(iii) Thank him for his forgiveness and all the other good things that come to mind.

(iv) Lastly, ask him to help others who need him and then ask him for your own needs.

Praying for your needs at the *end* instead of at the beginning is a good way of making sure your prayers are not selfish but more in line with what Jesus wants for you.

Dear Father, thank you for listening to all my prayers. Thank you for answering them, even when you say 'No'. Help me not to be sad when you do say 'No'. Help me to get to know you better. Help me to find out the things that please you. Amen.

Is prayer just coincidence?

One of the difficult things about following Jesus is that it can be very lonely. You might be the only person in your class who goes to church. And, if people know you're a Christian they might take it out on you. Even your friends might laugh it off. And maybe some of your relatives will tell you that it's just a religious phase that everybody goes through.

Following
Jesus

Well, Jesus didn't find it too easy either:

Read Mark 6:1–6

Jesus left that place and went back to his home town, followed by his disciples. On the Sabbath he began to teach in the synagogue. Many people were there; and when they heard him, they were all amazed. 'Where did he get all this?' they asked. 'What wisdom is this that has been given him? How does he perform miracles? Isn't he the carpenter, the son of Mary, and the brother of James, Joseph, Judas, and Simon? Aren't his sisters living here?' And so they rejected him. Jesus said to them, 'A prophet is respected everywhere except in his own home town and by his relatives and his family.' He was not able to perform any miracles there, except that he placed his hands on a few sick people and healed them. He was greatly surprised, because the people did not have faith.

The friends and neighbours that Jesus grew up with found it very difficult to take him seriously. Even though he did miracles and lived such a good life, they rejected him. Don't be surprised if people reject your Christian faith too. If they did it to Jesus they're even more likely to do it to you.

Jesus knows how hard it is for us. That's the reason why he's given us the Church—so Christians can help each other.

Lord Jesus, you know how difficult it is to be one of your followers. Thank you that I'm not on my own. Thank you that you're with me and that you know how it feels. Thank you for the others I know who also follow you. Amen.

> **Why do you think some people make fun of Christians?**

can be lonely

18

Do I have to go to church?

Do you have to go to football matches to be a football supporter?

Do you have to go to their concerts to be a fan of a pop group?
The answer, of course is 'No'. But you'd be missing out if you didn't go.
When people ask, 'Do I have to go to church to be a follower of Jesus?' the answer is 'No, but you'd be missing out by not going'.

Here's what 'Church' meant for the first Christians:

They spent their time in learning from the apostles (1), taking part in the fellowship (2), and sharing in the fellowship meals (3) and the prayers (4) . . . Day after day they met as a group in the Temple, and they had their meals together in their homes, eating with glad and humble hearts, praising God, and enjoying the good will of all the people . . . (5)

Acts of the Apostles 2.42, 46

So 'Church' means five things:
1 Learning about the Christian faith
2 Making friends with other Christians
3 Taking Holy Communion together
4 Praying together
5 Praising God together

The first Christians, although popular with ordinary people, faced a lot of opposition from the authorities. Meeting together helped them to keep on following Jesus. Sometimes they met in the temple (like a cathedral) and sometimes they met in each other's homes (perhaps like your church youth group). They became like a large family. That's how our churches should be—large families. Being a follower of Jesus, a member of the Church, should be like belonging to a family.

Lord, help me to see 'Church' as a family. Help me to feel part of that family. Amen.

19

How are people going to see Jesus today? They can't see him like they did 2000 years ago. People are now to see Jesus in those who follow him. Together we are Jesus to the world around us.

 This is how Paul explained it to the followers of Jesus who lived in Corinth:

All of you are Christ's body, and each one is a part of it.

1 Corinthians 12:27

Together we make up Christ's body in this world. Just as people saw God's love in Jesus now they are to see God's love in the followers of Jesus, the Church. We all have a part to play in this body. Imagine a body without a head, or a head without a nose! The body needs all its parts to do its job properly.

The first Christians had lots of arguments. Sometimes some of them would cut themselves off from others. It would be like refusing to go to church.

 This is how Paul tried to change their minds:

Christ is like a single body, which has many parts; it is still one body, even though it is made up of different parts. In the same way, all of us, whether Jews or Gentiles, whether slaves or free, have been baptized into one body by the same Spirit, and we have all been given the one Spirit to drink. For the body itself is not made up of only one part, but of many parts. If the foot were to say, 'Because I am not a hand, I don't belong to the body,' that would not keep it from being a part of the body.

1 Corinthians 12:12–15

Young people can feel that they don't really belong to the Church, especially if they find the services long and boring. But young people have a part to play in the Church. Older people may be the Church's head and shoulders but younger people can be its hands and feet. What things can you do in your church? Ask your minister or youth leader what sort of things you could do in the church. Here are some thoughts:

▷ **mowing and weeding the church grass**
▷ **visiting and shopping for housebound people**
▷ **delivering the magazine**
▷ **tidying up the church**
▷ **serving**
▷ **singing in the choir**

Add your own ideas to the list

....

....

....

....

Dear Lord, help me to see that I belong to the Church, the Body of Christ. Help me to see what part I can play in showing your love to those around. Amen.

Belonging to the Church

20

There's a lot wrong with the world. Violence, war and famine are just some of the terrible disasters we see reported on TV. Make a note here of some of the places where you know there are people suffering through war or famine:

....

....

These problems are the fault of human beings. There is enough food to feed everybody in the world but not everybody is given a fair share. Wars are started not by weapons but by the *people* who pull the triggers and push the buttons. The world is a cruel and unfair place because the people in it are cruel and unfair. Listen to what Jesus said about us:

Read Mark 7:21–23

> *For from the inside, from a person's heart, come the evil ideas which lead him to do immoral things, to rob, kill, commit adultery, be greedy, and do all sorts of evil things; deceit, indecency, jealousy, slander, pride, and folly—all these evil things come from inside a person and make him unclean.*

Although Jesus was referring to something else he's making the point that the root of the world's problems lies in the heart of each of us.

Now it's easy for us to blame other people like politicians and union leaders. But, we have to remember that every time we point a finger at someone else we point three back at ourselves. We're just the same as the people we blame. We're just as self-centred. If we were in their shoes we would probably act in just the same way. In fact if you want to see what's wrong with the world you don't have to look any further than in a mirror!

Lord Jesus, you know I'm no different from the people I blame for all the wars and famines in your world. Forgive me for the self-centredness that leads other people to go hungry and suffer. Help me to see what I can do now and in the future to make the world a fairer place. Amen.

The heart of the follower

Jesus asked his followers an important question:

'*Who do you say I am?*'
Peter answered,
'*You are the Messiah.*'

Read for yourself what happened in Mark 8:27–33.

('Messiah' is the Hebrew and 'Christ' is the Greek for our word 'anointed'.)

Peter and the disciples could see that Jesus was special. They knew that God had singled him out for a special task. Peter got it right that Jesus was God's anointed, the Messiah. But he got it wrong when it came to Jesus' special task. The disciples knew from the Old Testament that the Messiah would come and set up God's kingdom.

They thought wrongly that this would mean getting rid of the Roman army and putting a new king of the Jews in Jerusalem.

But God had other plans.

God wanted to set up his kingdom in the hearts of ordinary people. But first the sinful hearts had to be made clean. Through dying on the cross Jesus made it possible for our sins to be forgiven and for our hearts to be made clean and fit for a king.

Peter couldn't understand this at first. It was only later that he was able to figure it all out.

Lord Jesus, like Peter there's a lot that I do not understand. I know that you are God's special servant, the Messiah, the Christ. Help me each day to know you more clearly, to love you more dearly and to follow you more nearly. Amen.

The followers
realize

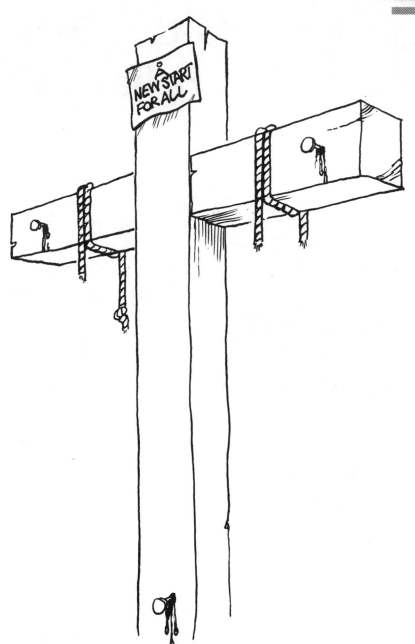

who Jesus is

Is the Bible reliable?

MANY HAVE BEEN UNDERTAKEN TO
DRAW UP AN ACCOUNT OF THE EVENTS
THINGS THAT HAVE BEEN
FULFILLED AMONG US, JUST AS
THEY WERE HANDED TO
THOSE WHO WERE, FROM
THE FIRST WERE EYE
AND SERVANT.

Nearly all that we know about God is in the Bible. It tells us about God and his Son, Jesus Christ. It was written by lots of different people who believed in God. The Old Testament was written in Hebrew by Jews. The New Testament was written in Greek by Jews who had become followers of Jesus. Some people can't be bothered with the Bible. They say it's just a lot of fairy tales.

This is how one of the Gospels begins:

Dear Theophilus: Many people have done their best to write a report of the things that have taken place among us. They wrote what we have been told by those who saw these things from the beginning and who proclaimed the message. And so, your Excellency, because I have carefully studied all these matters from their beginning, I thought it would be good to write an orderly account for you. I do this so that you will know the full truth about everything which you have been taught.

Luke 1:1–4

Luke wrote one of the four Gospels that tell us about Jesus. He does not start by saying 'Once upon a time'. The Gospel doesn't sound like a fairy story. Look at the passage again and try and sort out these words:

Luke tells Theophilus that lots of people had written PSTROER. They weren't fairy tales but a history of things that have PEHENAPD. They got their information from SESWEYINTESE. Luke carefully studied everything, he had been a thorough RHSRECAREE. His aim had been to VOCNIECN Theophilus. That's why he had written an orderly and CTRUAECA account.

Luke was writing about *facts*. He was trying to persuade people like Theophilus that the Christian faith was for them. The Gospel has stories about miracles. They're not easy to believe, not even in the first century. But, even though they were hard to believe, Luke mentions them because they happened. He had met the eyewitnesses who had seen them happen.

Lord, sometimes I find it hard to read the Bible. But I thank you for the Gospels that tell us about Jesus. Thank you that Luke studied everything so carefully before he wrote his Gospel. Thank you for speaking to me through it. As I read the Bible help me to see Jesus more clearly. And to know how to follow him better. Amen.

> **P.S.** Because we believe God speaks to us through the Bible, the reader in church will often say after a reading, 'This is the word of the Lord'; to which we all respond: 'Thanks be to God.'

The four Gospels don't take long to read. They're really quite small books. They don't tell us everything about Jesus. For example, we don't know what Jesus looked like, how tall he was, what clothes he wore. The writers were aware that they had left a lot out.

John says:

Now, there are many other things that Jesus did. If they were all written down one by one, I suppose that the whole world could not hold the books that would be written.

John 21:25

John and the others wrote and recorded certain facts and teachings about Jesus for a purpose:

In his disciples' presence Jesus performed many other miracles which are not written down in this book. But these have been written in order that you may believe that Jesus is the Messiah, the Son of God, and that through your faith in him you may have life.

John 20:30, 31

The purpose of the Gospels and the whole Bible is that we should know God's Son, Jesus Christ. God is to be seen and heard in his Son, Jesus. Jesus is to be seen and heard in the pages of the Bible. So, as we read the Bible we can say that it is here that we can see and hear God himself. That's why Christians say that the Bible is God's word to us.

The men and women of faith who wrote the books which make up the Bible were influenced by God's Spirit. So when we come to read it, either in church or in a group or on our own, we too should ask for the helpful influence of the Holy Spirit.

Lord, as I read the Bible and hear it being read, help me to listen to your voice speaking to me. Help me to understand the teachings of Jesus. Help me to be ready to change my habits. Help me with the Holy Spirit so that I may become more like Jesus. Amen.

The Bible
as God's word

In the master's service

of Man did not come to be served; he came to serve and to give his life to redeem many people.'

A question you're always being asked is 'What are you going to do when you grow up?' Many of us have dreams of being rich and famous like a pop star, actress or footballer.

The first followers had their dreams too. In fact they had a big argument as to who was going to have the best and most important job in God's kingdom.
When Jesus heard about it, this is what he said:

Read Mark 10:42–45

So Jesus called them all together to him and said, 'You know that the men who are considered rulers of the heathen have power over them, and the leaders have complete authority. This, however, is not the way it is among you. If one of you wants to be great, he must be the servant of the rest; and if one of you wants to be first, he must be the slave of all. For even the Son

Jesus, of all people, was entitled to be waited on hand and foot. But he came to serve others. He put other people before himself. He gave himself to helping people, especially the ones who were ignored by others, like the blind, the poor and the lepers.
Real greatness doesn't lie in being rich and famous and powerful. Real greatness lies in being a servant like Jesus. Put God first, others second and yourself last.
Think for a moment of someone at your school whom everyone looks down upon.
Does Jesus look down on him or her? Do you?
What practical steps could you take to help that person and treat him or her as Jesus would?

LONELY!

25

Jesus is king

If you wanted to change the world how would you go about it?

What would you need? Here are some suggestions:
▷ **A lot of money?**
▷ **A good education?**
▷ **Come from an influential family?**
▷ **A large army?**

And your own ideas:

....

....

Jesus came to change the world. And yet he had none of these things. He had little money. He could read and write but had

nothing like a college education. His parents had little influence. But even though he wasn't brought up in a palace ordinary people began to realize that Jesus was a king.

 Read Mark 11:1–10

The Jews knew from the Old Testament that their future king would one day ride into Jerusalem on the back of a donkey. So when they saw Jesus riding into Jerusalem in this way they got excited. Here was their king!

Just like the twelve disciples they didn't fully understand what sort of a king Jesus was. But they welcomed him enthusiastically.

Jesus is king of the world. Jesus rules over the whole earth. He is in control. Even when things seem out of control the Bible reminds us that he's got the whole world in his hands. So the world is God's kingdom.

Jesus is king of the Church. The Church is made up of individual people who have chosen to give Jesus free reign over their lives. So the Church too is God's kingdom. God's plan for changing the world is that more and more people should make Jesus their king. God wants the kingdom of his Church to spread throughout the kingdom of this world. That's why Jesus told us to pray: *'May your Kingdom come . . . on earth . . .'* How will this happen? Through you and all God's subjects.

Lord Jesus, you are king over every king, queen and president. May more and more people make you their king and so come into your Church. Help me to play my part in building your kingdom on earth. Amen.

Jesus is king of the whole world. Is your local church linked with a missionary in another part of God's world? Write his or her name here:

. . . .

Jesus' two commandments

The word 'love' can mean lots of different things. Here are some examples. Try and put the sentences in a different way:

I love hamburgers.   ....

I love my grandmother.   ....

I love football.   ....

I love my girlfriend/boyfriend.   ....

I love computers.   ....

I love God.   ....

Loving God is a different sort of love altogether.

Read what Jesus said about love in Mark 12:28–34.

The Ten Commandments can be boiled down to two: **love God** and **love your neighbour**.

Love God

Jesus said, '*Love the Lord your God with all your heart, with all your soul, with all your mind and all with your strength.*' But how can we love God when we can't even see him? We see God in the face of Jesus. So loving God means loving Jesus. We are called to love him in three ways:

1   With our **minds**—we use our *minds* to get to know him in the Gospels.
2   With our **feelings**—when we see how much he loves us we can start to *feel* good and *feel* love for him in return.
3   With our **wills**—even when we don't feel a thing we *will* go on putting him first in our lives by obeying his commandments.

Love your neighbour

It's easy to be kind to those who are kind to you. Christian love means loving *everybody*—all your neighbours, even the ones who are nasty to you.

Here are fourteen different groups of people. Put them into seven pairs:
Arabs, Whites, Capitalists, Catholics, Socialists, Bosses, Communists, Jews, Blacks, North, Protestants, South, Workers, Conservatives.
For example:

Conservatives   Socialists

....

....

....

....

....

....

Sometimes these groups in the pairs hate each other. When a person decides to follow Jesus he promises to love even his sworn enemy.

Lord Jesus, you know it is easy to love those who love you in return. Help me to love people I don't like. Help me to love even my sworn enemies. Amen.

Very often you'll hear people saying: 'I just don't know what the world is coming to.' Listen to some of the things Jesus had to say:

Read Mark 13:1–8

And don't be troubled when you hear the noise of battles close by and news of battles far away. Such things must happen, but they do not mean that the end has come.

Mark 13:7

Jesus tells the future

Jesus told his followers that the Temple in Jerusalem would disappear. So too the planet earth is bound one day to come to an end. But just how and when all this will happen, no one knows.

Christians should do all in their power to make peace and not war. But Jesus knows what people are like and tells us not to be surprised by what men and women will do to each other.

He tells his followers not to be alarmed and for one very good reason. There's more to life than living here on earth. Life with God will carry on long after this planet has disappeared.

28

In Jesus' time bread and wine were as common as potatoes and milk are to us. Jesus took these two ordinary things and made them very special.

Read what Jesus did in Mark 14:12–25.

Holy Communion –with Jesus

Paul wrote two letters to the church in Corinth. This comes from one of them:

For I received from the Lord the teaching that I passed on to you: that the Lord Jesus, on the night he was betrayed, took a piece of bread, broke it, and said, 'This is my body, which is for you. Do this in memory of me.' In the same way, after the supper he took the cup and said, 'This cup is God's new covenant, sealed with my blood. Whenever you drink it, do so in memory of me.' This means that every time you eat this bread and drink from this cup you proclaim the Lord's death until he comes.

1 Corinthians 11:23–26

Jesus took the bread and used it as a picture of the way he was giving his body to be crucified; he took the red wine and used it as a picture of how he would shed his own blood on the cross. Whenever the minister repeats these special words of Jesus over the bread and the wine they become for us Christ's body and blood, just as they did for the first followers of Jesus. They remind us of how he willingly died for us, for our forgiveness. Receiving the bread and the wine (sometimes called the 'elements', or the 'sacrament') is a special moment. It's like welcoming Jesus into our lives and saying, 'Thank you, dear Lord, for loving me so much that you died for me'. That's why we sometimes call the service the Eucharist, which comes from the Greek word 'Thank you'. We also call it 'communion' because that's when Christians, knowing their sins are forgiven, can come close to their master.

This is the prayer many pray after they have received the bread and the wine:

Almighty God, we thank you for feeding us with the body and blood of your Son Jesus Christ. Through him we offer you our souls and bodies to be a living sacrifice. Send us out in the power of your Spirit to live and work to your praise and glory. Amen.

Imagine for a moment that you had a large jar of sweets and you gave one each to everyone in your class. Your class would all have at least one thing in common—the sweet they had just eaten.

So too when at Holy Communion we all receive the bread and wine we have this in common with each other. It underlines that the Church is not a group of separate individuals but one body. In other words, mums and dads, children and grandparents, young and old, individuals and families, minister and people are all part of the one body of Christ the Church, eating and drinking the same bread and wine.

This is how Paul put it:

The cup we use in the Lord's Supper and for which we give thanks to God: when we drink from it, we are sharing in the blood of Christ. And the bread we break: when we eat it, we are sharing in the body of Christ. Because there is the one loaf of bread, all of us, though many, are one body, for we all share the same loaf.

1 Corinthians 10:16, 17

Holy Communion

This is why during the Communion Service we often have time to speak to each other and wish one another God's peace. It's a way of saying, 'We're one family!'

The Communion is two-way. Like a cross there is a line upwards that reminds us of our communion and friendship with God; and there is a line across which reminds us that we belong to each other. ←——→

This cross ←┼→ is at the centre

of our lives as followers of Jesus.

Think back to your last church service. Try to remember who sat next to you. Pray for them now:

Dear Lord, thank you that as followers of Jesus we belong to one family. Please bless . . . . and. . . . . Help them today to follow Jesus. Amen.

Next time you're in church try to remember to pray for those who sit next to you.

—with each other

Jesus dies and rises

When Jesus died Mark says that
the curtain in the Temple was torn
in two. This gives a picture and
another clue to what Jesus' death
means.

Read Mark 15:33–39

The Holy of Holies was the most holy place in the Temple. It was curtained off. Nobody was ever allowed in. The only exception was the High Priest. Once a year he went in to offer a sacrifice and to ask God's forgiveness for everybody's sins. The curtain was a picture of selfish men and women being cut off from the Holy God. When the curtain is torn it is Mark's visual aid to show us that with Jesus' sacrifice on the cross God and his people are reunited. Of course, that's not the end of the story.

 Read Mark 16:1–8

The Resurrection is difficult to believe. It's not the sort of thing we see every day. It was hard too for the first followers to believe. But they saw with their own eyes an empty tomb and Jesus alive. Perhaps we shouldn't be too surprised to see God bring his own Son through death to life again. It would be harder to see Jesus as God's Son if he had remained dead in the tomb!

All the people who wrote about the Resurrection and about Jesus being God's Son were, of course, Christians. In the end we've got only their word for it. But since they were ready to be killed for believing it we can be sure they had good reasons for believing it so firmly.

Lord Jesus, thank you that you are alive in your world, in your Church and with your people. Thank you that you are with me today. Thank you that you do not leave us to fend for ourselves. Help me to follow you, whatever the cost. Amen.

The first followers of Jesus believed in God. They looked on him as their Father. When they saw Jesus alive again after his crucifixion they were convinced that he must be God's Son. Then after Jesus left them they started to feel a power inside themselves. This power gave them the same courage and understanding that Jesus had given them.

Jesus and the Holy Spirit

It all began when they met together in Jerusalem for a Harvest Festival (Pentecost) when they were all filled with the Holy Spirit.

At your Confirmation the Bishop will lay hands on you and pray that you will be filled with the Holy Spirit. Here are two of the things the Holy Spirit does for us:

> 1 ...and no one can confess 'Jesus is Lord,' unless he is guided by the Holy Spirit
>
> 1 Corinthians 12:3

It is the Holy Spirit who helps us to follow Jesus. The desire in us to follow Jesus doesn't come from ourselves but from the influence of God's Spirit on us.

> 2 Jesus said, 'When, however, the Spirit comes, who reveals the truth about God, he will lead you into all the truth...'
>
> John 16:13

It is the Holy Spirit who helps us to understand the Christian faith. Whenever you feel you're understanding more, then that's a sign of God's Spirit influencing you.

If you find it hard to follow Jesus ask the Father for the help of the Holy Spirit.
If you find it difficult to understand Christianity ask the Father for the help of the Holy Spirit.

 At your Confirmation the Bishop will ask you:

'Do you believe and trust in his Holy Spirit, who gives life to the people of God?'

You will answer:
'I believe and trust in him.'

Pray this prayer for yourself. It's taken from the one the Bishop (and the whole congregation) will pray for you:

Defend, O Lord, your servant with your heavenly grace, that I may continue yours for ever, and daily increase in your Holy Spirit more and more, until I come to your everlasting kingdom. Amen.

If you have enjoyed using *Following Jesus*, you might like to look at other titles in the series.

Serving Jesus tackles many of the questions and problems facing young people as they try to serve Jesus. A further 27 units are presented, each linked with a character or event from the New Testament and including a short Bible reading and prayer. *Serving Jesus* will be particularly suitable for those who have just been confirmed. Price: £1.95 per copy

Praying with Jesus presents 28 units which each explore one aspect of 'praying with Jesus', with a Bible reading, comment and short assignment. *Praying with Jesus* will appeal to confirmation and post-confirmation candidates and any person anxious to learn more about prayer. Price: £1.95 per copy.

Another 9 titles are planned in the *Following Jesus* series. The first of these, *The Power of Jesus* and *Images of Jesus in John* should be published in September 1993.

All titles in the series are illustrated throughout by Taffy.

Serving Jesus and *Praying with Jesus*

are available now from all good Christian Bookshops, or in case of difficulty from BRF, Peter's Way, Sandy Lane West, Oxford, OX4 5HG. If ordering direct from BRF please add 15% (minimum 85p) to cover post and packing.

If you would like to know more about the full range of Bible reading notes and other Bible reading and group study materials published by the Bible Reading Fellowship, write and ask for a free catalogue.

Text copyright © James Jones 1984, 1993

Illustrations copyright © Taffy 1993

The author asserts the moral right to be identified as the author of this work

Published by
The Bible Reading Fellowship
Peter's Way
Sandy Lane West
Oxford
OX4 5HG
ISBN 0 7459 2579 0

First published 1984
Reprinted 1986, 1989, 1991, 1992
This edition 1993
All rights reserved

Acknowledgments

Bible text is reproduced from the Good News Bible published by the Bible Societies/HarperCollins

Material from The Alternative Service Book 1980 is copyright © and reproduced by kind permission of the Central Board of Finance of the Church of England

A catalogue record for this book is available from the British Library

Printed and bound in Slovenia